SUPER CUTE FARTING ANIMALS

Find out more about M.T. Lott at:
mtlottbooks.com
www.facebook.com/authormtlott

Hedgies like little tushy ticklers...

A foal has a real barn burner!

Bunny farts are pootie cute!

Happy Corgi cheek squeaks!

Watch out for the wise
owl's air biscuit...

A sloth's fart is a slow floater....

Visit
mtlottbooks.com
to join my email list and
get your free coloring pages!

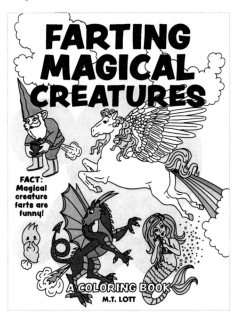

CPSIA information can be obtained
at www.ICGtesting.com
Printed in the USA
LVOW09s0050070518
576240LV00030BA/424/P